OneNote

Discover How To Easily Become More Organized, Productive & Efficient With Microsoft OneNote

By Ace McCloud
Copyright © 2015

Disclaimer

The information provided in this book is designed to provide helpful information on the subjects discussed. This book is not meant to be used, nor should it be used, to diagnose or treat any medical condition. For diagnosis or treatment of any medical problem, consult your own physician. The publisher and author are not responsible for any specific health or allergy needs that may require medical supervision and are not liable for any damages or negative consequences from any treatment, action, application or preparation, to any person reading or following the information in this book. Any references included are provided for informational purposes only. Readers should be aware that any websites or links listed in this book may change.

Table of Contents

DEDICATED TO THOSE WHO ARE PLAYING THE GAME OF LIFE TO

KEEP ON PUSHING AND NEVER GIVE UP!

Ace McCloud

Be sure to check out my website for all my Books and Audio books.

www.AcesEbooks.com

Introduction

I want to thank you and congratulate you for buying the book, "OneNote: Discover How To Easily Become More Organized, Productive & Efficient With Microsoft OneNote."

Microsoft OneNote is a powerful piece of software that is often referred to as an "all-in-one" digital notebook. You can use OneNote in a variety of ways, such as writing down your thoughts, ideas, tasks and you can even use it to jot down sketches or to write out mathematical equations. What makes OneNote better than a regular notebook is that you can keep all of your important information in one safe place. With OneNote, you will never have to worry about keeping stacks and stacks of notebooks ever again. You will never have to manually divide sections of your notebooks for different subjects and you will never have to worry about losing your notes or having them get all mixed together. You will never have to pay for single notebooks again (and you probably know how expensive that can get!). Best of all, everything is digital, so you will never have to worry about ruining the environment, either.

OneNote has been around since 2003, although the 2010 version has gained the most popularity and is the most developed besides the 2013 version. Since its release, many people who have discovered this hidden gem have been able to reinvent their organizational skills and become more effective at what they do. I call it a hidden gem because most schools don't teach this program along with the other Microsoft office programs such as the more popular Word and PowerPoint. OneNote has revolutionized my business and can't recommend it enough! All you will ever need with OneNote is a computer, a keyboard and yourself. If you are not familiar with or have never heard of Microsoft OneNote, here is a quick YouTube video about the program: The Wonders of Microsoft OneNote 2010 by Itech Insights.

It is the perfect program for students, businesspeople, creative thinkers, professors, scientists, doctors and nearly anyone in any field. No matter how much information you need to store, OneNote has unlimited space for you to do so. OneNote comes with many features (most of which you will learn later on in this book), but one of its biggest features is that you can synchronize your digital notebooks with any device you have, giving you 24/7 access to your notes and other valuable information wherever you are, whatever time of the day. The fact that you can connect your digital notebook to the internet also opens many doors for collaboration and communication among industries and leaders. For example, a group of students in a class can use OneNote's connectivity features to collaborate online or a group of business professionals could use it to collaborate for a meeting.

Another huge feature of OneNote is that it is designed to help you stay more organized throughout the day. Many of the functions contained within this program are made so that you can get your life in order, allowing you more room for success and production. Once you've mastered the organizational features of OneNote, you will never have to worry about keeping notes together, losing pages or having to mark certain pages for future reference.

The world is rapidly moving toward a digital online era and having a powerful program like OneNote as your ally will give you a great advantage! Although you may enjoy traditional notebooks, you may slowly find yourself falling behind without a technological program such as OneNote. This program is so popular that it is now a part of all Microsoft product packages including Microsoft Office Home and Student 2010 as well as the newer packages for Windows 8+. Don't fall behind and miss out on any opportunities for productivity, efficiency and most of all: success!

This book contains proven steps and strategies on how to become a master at OneNote so that you can stay on top of your game, no matter what you use it for. OneNote is a powerful program that is easy to learn and contains many features and functions which can make your life so much better. This book will guide you through OneNote's in an easy to understand step-by-step manner so that you can learn every aspect of this wonderful program. There is also in-depth explanations of basic functions for those who may have never learned Microsoft office at all or those who just need a good refresher.

If you already have the program, I highly recommend having it open as you read this book so that you can follow along and interact. By doing this, you are twice as likely to memorize each function and what it does, allowing you to become proficient in this program at a faster rate. My life has changed for the better ever since I started using this program and I am sure you will be quite pleased at how much more organized and productive you can be from using it. I wish you the best of luck and I hope that Microsoft OneNote brings as much joy into your life as it has in mine.

Chapter 1: Getting to Know OneNote

Let's get started! The first thing you should do when you open OneNote is to create a new notebook. You can do this by clicking File->New. Then you will be prompted to select where you want to save your notebook. The program will give you the options to save it on the web, on a network or on your computer. The benefit of saving your notebook onto the web or network is that you can share it with others. However, you can save your notebook to your computer for private access, which is what I do.

Next, the program will ask you to name your notebook. You will see a blank box where you can click and type in anything you want. Some examples would be "Business" or "Personal". Below that, you will get to customize where OneNote saves your notebook. If you chose to save it on the web, you will get to select which publically shared folder on your drive you want to save it in. If you want to share it on a network, you will be able to type the network into a blank box. If you opt to make it a private notebook, it will ask you what folder you want to save it in on your hard drive.

At the bottom of the screen, you will then see a little box that says "Create Notebook." Simply click on that to get started!

Functions and Features

OneNote contains many useful functions and features, all of which you will learn about in depth throughout this book. However, to familiarize you with the basics of how OneNote works, let's start from the top.

At the very top of the program (where you see the little purple icon for OneNote in the top left-hand corner), you will see 4 clickable icons. The first clickable icon is a straight arrow pointing to the left. This is the **Back Button**. You can use this button to scroll through the sections of your notebook (you will learn about sections in a little bit). Next to the back arrow is another arrow that looks like it's turning backwards. That is your **Undo Button**. If you make a mistake or type something that you decided to erase, you can click this button to undo your last action. You can usually click the undo button a few times to erase your last couple of actions, but it only goes back so far. Be sure you remember this button as it is very useful.

After the undo button, you will see an icon that looks like a square with one side highlighted. That is the **Dock to Desktop** icon. The dock to desktop icon is one of the best features of this program. When you click on it, OneNote will automatically dock to the right-hand side of your screen. This allows you to continue using OneNote or have it off to the side where you can refer to it while using other programs, such as Internet Explorer. To undock OneNote, simply click on the same button again.

When you undock OneNote, it will go back to full-screen mode. The icon to the right of the dock button is the **Full Page View** icon. This feature can be useful for studying or reading your notes without having any distractions on your screen. Remember, in full screen mode you cannot see your other notebooks on the left hand side, so click the full screen mode button again if you want to access your other notebooks.

Now turn your attention to the next row of tools. Underneath the icons you just learned about, you will see 7 different tabs labeled "File," "Home," "Insert," "Share," "Draw," "Review," and "View."

The **File** tab is self-explanatory. By clicking on File, you will be able to sync your notebooks, open a pre-existing notebook, create a new notebook, share your notebook, save it as a different file name, send it through email or to another application, print pages in it or access the built-in help features. You will also have the option to customize some of the program settings under the tab. Finally, you can exit the program by clicking the exit button all the way at the bottom. Be sure to keep a manual backup for yourself as well on an external hard drive or on the cloud. This is easy to do by going to File then Options then clicking on Save and Backup.

The **Home** tab allows you to switch back to the main screen where you can manage and edit your notebook. The **Insert** tab contains many useful features. Under this tab, you can insert spaces, tables, pictures, screen grabs, hyperlinks, audio/video recordings, timestamps and symbols to the pages of your notebook. This is very easy to do with OneNote and is a main reason why people love it so much. You can also copy/paste your favorite links and pictures into OneNote to easily organize your favorite places and things.

Underneath the **Share** tab, you have the option of sharing your notebook and/or single pages via email. You can also use this tab to search for recent edits that another user may have made. You can also access the Notebook Recycle Bin to see the history of changes for your shared notebook.

Next to the share tab is the **Draw** tab, another very powerful feature of OneNote. Under this tab, you have the option of writing in your notebook freehand (useful for those with a pen and tablet hook-up), highlighting important notes and even doing math in your notebook. You will discover just how great this feature is as well as the usefulness of the insert tab in just a few chapters.

Under the **Review** tab, you can check your notebook for spelling errors, research a topic in the sidebar or translate your pages. Finally, the **View** tab allows you to customize how you want the program to look and to feel. You can select this tab to view your notebook in full-screen mode or in regular view. You can also use the zoom in/out feature here as well as select the page color, add ruled lines and open up another window.

Getting To Know Your Notebook

Now that you have discovered how the basic functions of OneNote work, the next step for you is to familiarize yourself with the notebook screen. **At this point, it is important for you to know that OneNote has an automatic save feature, which is why there is no regular "Save" option under the File tab.** Have no worries, all of your data is getting saved as soon as you put it in! Now let's move on to your actual notebook, where you will be spending the most time in this program.

Starting all the way on the left-hand side of the screen, you may see different tabs. These tabs represent the different notebooks that you have saved to your computer. So if you have two notebooks, one labeled "School" and one labeled "Work," you can switch between those two notebooks by simply clicking on them in the left-hand side of the screen. Next you will notice your page, where you can write notes and above your blank page you will see a tab. If you've started a new notebook, the tab will read **New Section 1.** Remember when you used to buy those color-coded dividers for your school binders? The tabs (known as **Sections**) that are above your page represent those. For example, if you used OneNote for school, you could have multiple tabs reading "English," "Biology," "Algebra," and "Homework." You can add sections to your notebook by simply clicking on the starburst icon next to each section tab. To rename the section, simply double-click on the tab.

Now focus your attention to the right. You will see a section of the program called **Pages.** This is where you can create new pages to each notebook you've created. For example, let's say you have your "school" notebook open as well as your "homework" section. The pages function allows you to have multiple pages under that section. You can have a page for each day of the week. To add a new page to a section of your notebook, simply click **New Page**. You can make a **Subpage** by right-clicking on the page tab and selecting "Make Subpage." You can also move/rearrange pages by right-clicking on the page tab and selecting "Move or Copy."

Exploring Your Pages

Every time you add a new page, OneNote will automatically put a timestamp on it, noting the date as well as the time the page was created. Above the timestamp, you will see a small rectangular box where you can add a title to your page. For example (going off our running example of a school notebook), you could write "Homework for Monday" as the title. Once you've hit enter, OneNote will bring you down to the page and open a box where you can start writing.

You can type as much as you want into this box—it will automatically grow. One cool thing about OneNote is that you can have as many text boxes as you want and you can move them around. Go ahead and try it—write in one box and then click outside of the box to exit. Then click in another area on the page and start writing again. You will notice that the new text is contained in a new box. When you hold the mouse over it, you will see a thin gray bar on top. By clicking on that bar, you can move each text box around wherever you want. I think this feature is best for when you're doing brainstorming because it gives you ultimate control over your page content. It's also great for To Do lists and many other things, as you can easily move important items to the top of the list and less essential things to the bottom. It's also very handy for keeping things alphabetically organized!

Last but not least, there is a small search bar in the top right-hand corner of the screen, right above the area where you can create new pages. You can use this search bar to search for text within every notebook that you have. You don't even have to have a notebook open to be able to search for a term. You can opt to search all notebooks or you can isolate it to searching just one. You can also choose to search individual sections or pages. Simply type in the term or phrase you're looking for and OneNote will tell you where to locate it. You can also click on the notebook where the term or phrase is located to open it. My favorite way to search is to just go to the section of the notebook where I know the information is at and then hit CTRL + F, which is the shortcut to search the current page.

Chapter 2: Unlocking the True Power of Organization with OneNote

In OneNote, there are many useful options and features under the Home tab that you can use to make your notes more organized and coherent. I will take you through every option under the Home tab in this chapter and explain how to use it to your best advantage.

Starting all the way from the left, you will see the **Paste** icon. By clicking on that icon, OneNote will paste in the last piece of text that you've highlighted and cut/copied from your computer. This function is helpful for when you're copying words from your internet browser or another application such as Microsoft word. If you are copying from one place to one note, you can use the shortcut of CTRL +C to copy and CTRL + V to Paste. Next to the Paste icon are the **Cut** and **Copy** icons. These features are useful for when you're working and editing within OneNote. You can highlight a piece of your text and "cut" it, meaning it disappears from the page but can be reinserted with the Paste button. You can also "copy" your text and duplicate it elsewhere in your notebook. When you highlight and copy your text, it doesn't disappear. Underneath the cut and copy buttons is the **Format Painter** button. The Format Painter option allows you to copy formatting from one place in your notebook and apply it to another section of text.

To the right of the Cut, Copy and Paste options box is the section where you can customize your text. You will see a font drop-down box where you can change the font type of your text. The default font in OneNote 2010 is Calibri. Next to the font drop-down box is another drop-down box where you can change the size of your font. Underneath those boxes, you will see 5 small icons that will allow you to further customize your text. Starting from the right, there is the **Bold** option, which allows you to make all or some of your text bold-faced. Next is the **Italics** option, *which can make your font look like this*. Third is the **Underline** option, <u>which can make your text look like this.</u> Fourth is the **Strikethrough** option, ~~which can make your text look like this.~~ Finally, there is the **Subscript/Superscript** option, which can make your text look like this $_{or this.}$

Looking back up next to the font drop-down boxes, you will see a few more functions. The next two icons are **Bullet Functions**. The first one allows you to put your text next to bullets and the following one lets you bullet it with letters/numbers instead of small black circles. Under the first bullet icon, there is a small arrow that opens up another drop-down box. If you click on that arrow, you will see that you can customize how your bullets look. You can choose anything from arrows to snowflakes to smiley faces. If you do the same for the second icon, you will see that you have the option to change the lettering into roman numerals, written words or interchangeable icons. Finally, the last icon up top you will see is an icon with two A's in a box next to an eraser. This is the **Clear Formatting** icon. By clicking on this icon while you have a piece of modified text highlight (bolded, italicized, bulleted, etc.) you can instantly undo the formatting and change it back to normal.

Underneath those icons and next to the text customization icons, you will see 5 more icons for that section. The first icon bears a bright yellow color and is the **Text Highlight Color** option. When you highlight a piece of text and click on that icon your text will get highlighted in the desired color. This can be a very useful feature when taking notes because you can highlight the most important parts. Next to the Text Highlight Color icon you will see the letter A with a black strip underneath it. This is the **Font Color** button and it enables you to change the color of your font. You will see a drop-down arrow next to this icon and, when clicked, you can pick any color you would like for your text. At the very top of the drop-down box, you can click "automatic color" to change your text back to its default color.

The next three icons are paragraph formatting options. The first two icons are the **Decrease Paragraph Indent** and **Increase Paragraph Indent** buttons. By clicking at the beginning of a paragraph, you can either move it in or out, thus decreasing or increasing the indent level. In the next box over you will see that you can stylize your text by using different preset **Headings**. These headings are pre-made and meant to make your life easier because you can use them to break up different sections of your notes. The drop-down box shows you the different sized headings you can use. Heading 1 is the largest font and Heading 6 is the smallest. This box also gives you the option to format your text for a citation, code, quote or page title. You can also set your text style back to normal.

After the style box you will discover one of the most important and unique features of OneNote—the **Tags**. By looking at the tabs box and expanding it, you will see many different icons with different labels (such as to-do, important, etc.). One of the coolest things is that you can use these different tags throughout your notes to take even more notes! For example, if you have written a to-do list in the middle of your notes, you can tag that list with the to-do icon to break it up and make it stand out. Best of all, you can click the little square next to each task as you complete it and a check will appear in the box, noting that you've completed the task. You can tag questions with a "?" symbol, you can mark text as important with a little yellow star and you can even tag ideas with a little lightbulb symbol, which I think is perfect for brainstorming.

There is almost a tag for anything you can think of, including one for contacts, addresses, phone numbers, website links, passwords, and reminders. You can drop these symbols anywhere in your notebook to make your notes more organized and effective. You can also create custom tags. To create a custom tag, expand the tab drop-down box and go all the way to the bottom where it says "Customize Tags." A box will then pop up, enabling you to create your own tag and pick an icon. You can also modify an existing tag to suit your needs.

Next to the tag box, you will discover the **Find Tags** function, where you can search all tags throughout all of your notebooks. This is useful for ensuring that you've checked off everything on your to-do list, answered all important questions and have contacted everyone you need to see, etc. Think of the Find Tags function as your "double-check box." You can always see what you need to complete on hand with this tool. Finally, the last function under the Home Tab is the **Email Page** option. By clicking on that icon, you can email the page you're working on through Outlook.

Chapter 3: Making the Most of Insert Options

Now that you have seen all the great things you can do with OneNote under the Home tab, it is time to discover the great and useful features under the Inserts tab. Like its name reads, many of the features under this tab can be "inserted" into your pages for optimal organization and note-taking. Many of these features are unique to OneNote and awesome in functionality!

Start by clicking on the **Insert tab** to the right of the Home tab. Starting all the way on the left, you will find a very unique tool called the **Insert Space** function. Have you ever taken notes in a ruled notebook only to find yourself wishing you could just add more spaces in between? With the Insert Space function, you can now do that in OneNote! To make more space on your page, simply click that icon and hover it over a section in your notes. You will notice a thin, blue horizontal line or a vertical line if you hover near the edge. Simply click and drag your notes to the right or down. Any text to the right or below the line will magically move all at once! It's almost like magic.

Next to the Insert Space function, you will see the **Table** function. If you've ever used another Microsoft program such as Microsoft Word, you should easily be able to learn how to use the Table function. Simply click on the icon and create a quick table by selecting its size. Once your table has been created, a special toolbar will appear where you can further modify it (add/delete rows or columns, select sections of your table, etc.) Once your table has been created, you can move it around your page by clicking on the thin gray bar on the top and dragging it around.

The two following features are unique in their functionality and can really help you get serious about note taking. Next to the Table function are the **Images** options. You're probably familiar with how to insert an image into Word or PowerPoint. It's pretty much the same process for this program too. Simply click on the Picture icon and browse for a picture on your hard drive to put in your notes. However, the **Screen Clipping** tool, located directly next to the Picture icon is what really gives OneNote an upper advantage. The Screen Clipping tool allows you to do a screen grab and insert it into your page. If you click on the icon, OneNote will temporarily minimize, allowing you to select a region of your screen to grab. This can be useful for copying information off websites, copying someone else's notes, copying pictures off the web, etc. Every time you do a screen clipping, OneNote will also insert a time-stamp with the image so you can know when exactly you inserted it into your notebook.

The next icon is the **Link** tool. By clicking on this icon you can add a hyperlink anywhere on your page. Additionally, you can link to another page in another notebook within OneNote when using this tool. After the Link tool you will see the files section. Here, you have the **Attach File**, **File Printout** and **Scanner Printout** functions. The Attach File function simply allows you to attach a file from your hard drive anywhere in your notebook. The File Printout Scanner

Printout functions allow you to attach files to your notebook that have been scanned in or downloaded. One really unique feature of OneNote is that you can search your notebook for these files for instant access.

The next set of functions you will see are some of the best kept secrets of OneNote. Next to the file attachment options you will see two icons for recording video and audio called **Record Audio** and **Record Video**. As long as you have a built-in microphone and/or webcam, (or an attachable one), you can record your voice and movement and insert it directly into your notebook. This is a great option for many things. Students may find the audio function useful for taking notes in a huge lecture and businesspeople may find the video function useful for journaling about their ideas. Many people would rather store their information through audio and video rather than words, so OneNote can definitely win over many people. As with text, you can drop the audio/video files anywhere in your notebook and play them directly back on your computer at any time. It's always nice to have a section dedicated to your favorite videos or video links so you can easily have access to all your favorite things to watch!

The next set of tools, the timestamp options, is pretty simple. By clicking on the **Date** icon, OneNote will automatically insert the current date into your page. By clicking on the **Time** icon, OneNote will automatically insert the current time into your page. By clicking on the **Date & Time** icon the program will automatically insert both the date and the time.

The final set of tools is the symbol tools. You will see these icons next to the timestamp features. By clicking on the **Insert Equation** icon OneNote will insert a mathematical equation into your notebook. By selecting the drop-down arrow you will see a set of preselected equations that you can insert, such as the Pythagorean Theorem. At the bottom of the drop down box is an option where you can insert your own custom equation. When you select that option, the toolbar at the top will change, giving you access to mathematical symbols and the ability to make special characters such as fractions, scripts and radicals among more. Next to the Insert Equation tool is the **Insert Symbol** icon. By clicking on this icon, you can insert various symbols into your page such as smiley faces, mailbox icons and more mathematical symbols. If you change the selected font to Wingdings, you can scroll through all the various symbols and insert them that way instead of having to type out each corresponding letter.

Chapter 4: Utilizing the Draw Tab

Now that you've gotten the chance to explore the Home and Insert tabs, it is time to check out the amazing features of OneNote under the Draw tab. The Draw tab is unique to OneNote because no other Microsoft program currently comes with this creative feature. People who find it easier to draw out ideas rather than write them out in words will love this. The Draw feature is best used with a third-party drawing tablet (you can usually hook it right into your computer), or if you have a touchscreen laptop and a stylus, but even if you don't have any of those tools you can still make the most of it.

The first icon all the way at the far left of the toolbar is the Select and Type icon. Clicking on this button allows you to go back to the default settings where you can click on the page and start typing text. Next you will see an eraser icon with a sun shining behind it. This is the Eraser tool and it will come in very handy once you start using the draw ability. Underneath the Eraser icon you will see a drop-down arrow. By clicking on that arrow, you will get to select from a set of predefined erasers. By default, the eraser is set to Stroke, which means it will erase the last object you drew just by clicking on any part of it. You can also change it to a small, medium or large eraser where you have to hold the mouse button down to make erasures.

Next to the Select and Type and Eraser tool you will see the Lasso Select tool and the Panning Hand tool. The Lasso Select tool enables you to select regions of ink that you've drawn in freeform and the Panning Hand tool enables you to "grab" the page with your mouse and move it freely in any direction.

After these four icons is the true treasure of OneNote: the pens. In the middle of the toolbar you will see 14 boxes, all of which contain the image of a pen or highlighter with ink trailing out of it. The drop-down box extends the pen options and you can choose from different sizes. At the bottom of the drop-down box you will see where it says "More Color & Thickness Options." By clicking on that box, you can further customize the size and color of your pen. In this section, you will also notice the Highlighter pen option. Like its name, this pen acts just like a highlighter. You can go to a page where you have typed text and run the highlighter over it. Instead of covering the text like a normal paintbrush, the highlighter will just make the text stand out. This tool is helpful for marking important notes and topics, especially when you have a lot of information on hand. The default highlighter colors are yellow, turquoise, neon green and purple, but you can customize it to be anything you want under More Color & Thickness Options.

Next to the pens you will see the Shapes box, which contains the perfect tools for geometry and graphing. By clicking on the various icons in this box, you can add professional shapes to your pages. Most of the shapes in this box are geometrical symbols such as lines, squares, circles, parallelograms, triangles, diamonds and shapes to build graphs. If you're taking a math class or going to be figuring out mathematical equations this is the perfect toolbox for you to utilize. This function may even be helpful for small business owners who need to put their numbers in a visual format. Next to the Shapes box you will see another Color & Thickness tool where you can manipulate the thickness and color of the shapes you make.

The Insert Space icon makes another appearance under the Draw tab so that you can conveniently move your shapes and other notes around to make it easier to manage your pages. If you click on your shapes, you will also notice that you can delete them or arrange them on top/behind each other by using the Delete and Arrange tools that are located next to the Insert Space icon. The Arrange tool is helpful for cases when you need to create a double-bar graph or a circle comparison chart. Next to the Arrange icon is the Rotate icon, which allows you to rotate a selected shape anywhere from a 45 degree angle, a 90 degree angle or horizontally/vertically.

The last two tools under the Draw tab are really amazing and unique to OneNote. The first of the last two tools is the **Ink to Text** icon. This button allows you to turn handwritten text that you may have entered into OneNote into computerized text. For example, if you use the pen tool to write "Hello" in freehand, you can select that phrase and hit Ink to Text and then see it magically turn into "Hello" in text form. This tool can be really helpful if you're taking handwritten notes (preferably on a tablet for the most ease) and you need to sharpen/clean it up to share with others. Turning handwritten notes into text can also help you if you need to search for terms within your notes.

The last tool is the **Ink to Math** tool. Similar to the Ink to Text tool, this function can turn handwritten mathematical equations into professional text. Go ahead and try it—click on the Ink to Math Tool. Write out 2+2=4 in the space it presents to you and click Insert. The writing space grows with the equation so you never have to worry about running out of space. The Ink to Math tool is perfect for doing math in OneNote when you do not see an equation you need under the Insert tab or when you just need to work with a lot of different numbers.

Chapter 5: Using OneNote for Maximum Productivity

OneNote, as I am sure you have determined by now, is the perfect platform for boosting your productivity. Its main features are great for getting your days in order and helping you organize yourself, but this program is also designed to make your life more efficient. In this chapter, you will discover ways to make your life even better with OneNote and you will also learn about some more awesome features that may be helpful to you.

Top Feature #1

You can take notes with OneNote without even having to keep the program open. OneNote comes with two keyboard shortcuts that allow you to take quick notes. By hitting the Windows key and "N," a new page in OneNote will automatically open up and you can immediately start taking notes. When you take a note like this, OneNote will save it to your "Unfiled Notes" and you can go back and organize them later.

Another cool trick is that you can take an instant screenshot of your desktop and save it to one of your notebooks. This is useful for bookmarking information that you may need to use later. To take a screenshot simply hold the Windows key and S at the same time. The screen will go grey and a plus sign will appear. You want to highlight the entire area that you want to take a screen shot of. Once that is done, you will be given the option of where to save this picture in OneNote.

Top Feature #2

OneNote comes with preinstalled keyboard shortcuts that you can use to activate certain features without having to search for them within the program. Once you learn these keyboard shortcuts, odds are you will be able to store them in your memory and using them will become second nature over time. Once they become second nature they will be able to help you work much more quickly and efficiently.

Here is a list of the most helpful keyboard shortcuts in OneNote:

Ctrl+M **Open New Window**

Ctrl+Alt+D **Dock Window**

Ctrl+Z **Undo** (universal)

Ctrl+Y **Redo**

Ctrl+A **Select All** (universal)

Ctrl+ Period (.) **Apply or Remove Bullets**

Ctrl+K **Insert Link**

Ctrl+C **Copy Formatting**

Ctrl+V **Paste Formatting**

Ctrl+X **Cut Selection** (universal)

Ctrl+V **Paste Selection** (universal)

Ctrl+B **Bold Text or Undo Bold Text**

Ctrl+I **Italics or Undo Italics**

Ctrl+U **Underline Text or Undo Underline Text**

Shift+Enter **Insert Line Break**

Ctrl+Alt+1 **Apply Heading 1 to Text**

Ctrl+Alt+2 **Apply Heading 2 to Text**

Ctrl+Alt+3 **Apply Heading 3 to Text**

Ctrl+Alt+4 **Apply Heading 4 to Text**

Ctrl+Alt+5 **Apply Heading 5 to Text**

Ctrl+Alt+6 **Apply Heading 6 to Text**

F7 Key **Spell Check**

F11 Key **Toggle Full Page View**

Shift+F7 Key **Open Thesaurus**

Shift+F10 Key **Open Context Menu**

Ctrl+Shift+W **Execute Selected Operation on Toolbar**

Ctrl+1 **Toggle "To-Do" Tag**

Ctrl+2 **Toggle "Important" Tag**

Ctrl+3 **Toggle "Question" Tag**

Ctrl+4 **Toggle "Remember" Tag**

Ctrl+0 **Remove All Tags**

Ctrl+R **Align Paragraph to Right**

Ctrl+L **Align Paragraph to Left**

Ctrl+Shift+> **Make Font Size Bigger**

Ctrl+Shift+< **Make Font Size Smaller**

Ctrl+Shift+R **Toggle Ruled Lines**

Ctrl+N+F **Insert File to Page**

Ctrl+Alt+P **Playback Audio/Video**

Ctrl+Alt+Y **Rewind Audio/Video**

Ctrl+Alt+U **Fast Forward Audio/Video**

Ctrl+Shift+E **Email Page**

Alt+Shift+1 **Insert Time/Date Timestamp**

Alt+= **Insert Math Equation**

Alt+Shift+Up Arrow **Move Selected Text Up**

Alt+Shift+Down Arrow **Move Selected Text Down**

Home Key **Go to Beginning of Line**

End Key **Go to End of Line**

Page Up Key **Scroll Up Page**

Page Down Key **Scroll Down Page**

Ctrl+End **Jump to Bottom of Page**

Ctrl+F **Search Page**

Ctrl+E **Search All Notebooks**

Top Feature #3

With OneNote, you can compile a notebook of important handwritten or foreign documents for ultimate organization. For example, using the Inserts tab, you can scan and file receipts, notes, recipes, newspaper articles, book chapters, etc. and have them all in one simple file for quick access. With the audio/video feature, you can also enable a text search so that you can sit back and record things and then search for important words later on. You can enable the audio/video search feature by going to audio and video under options. **Bonus Tip:** If you have a tablet that connects to your computer, you can utilize the draw functions to take handwritten notes over anything you scan.

Top Feature #4

Templates are always a helpful shortcut and luckily OneNote has them. To view the notebook templates in OneNote, head over to the left hand side of the screen where you can see/add pages. Click on the drop-down arrow next to where it says "New Page" and select **Page Templates.** This will open up a window where you can view all the available templates. For your convenience, OneNote has broken down the categories of templates for students and business. The Academic templates can be really beneficial for students who want to organize their notes and the business templates are perfect for anyone who needs to plan for a meeting. There are many customizable options under the decorative category, all of which are perfect for giving your notebook a personal feel. The planner templates come with pre-organized checklists that are great for jumping right into your tasks and the blank templates offer a little more personalization with a basic feel.

Top Feature #5

The fifth top feature of OneNote is integration with other Microsoft programs. Specifically, Outlook and OneNote have a lot of integration features that can really boost your productivity (provided that you regularly use both of these programs). You can save content directly from Outlook into OneNote by looking for the "Send to OneNote" icon in Outlook. As you discovered previously in this book, you also know that you can send notebooks and pages in OneNote to Outlook. Whenever you send an email through OneNote, the program will add a footnote at the end that notes which program the content came from. You can customize this footnote by going under the Advanced Options settings and typing in a custom message.

The Send to OneNote or Email through Outlook features can be especially useful to those who deal with a lot of people daily. One idea is to store information, such as frequently asked questions or other informative documents and just send them out to clients when the information is requested.

You can also integrate OneNote with Microsoft Word. You can link your notes in OneNote to Word to avoid any excess copy-and-pasting. To link OneNote and Word, open Word and make sure that your document is saved in DOCX. Click on the Review tab and you will see a button in the toolbar that says Linked Notes. When you click on that button, a box will open up, asking you to select the notebook in which you want to save the linked notes. You can also do this with PowerPoint. Check out this tutorial, <u>Linking Notes in One Note</u> by InnovativeTeach, to learn more about this feature.

Top Feature #6

In OneNote, you can also change the type and feel of the "paper" you are writing on. Under the View tab you will see an icon that says Ruled Lines. By clicking on this icon, you will be able to select different types of "paper" from a drop-down box, such as ruled lines or grids. This can be useful if you're used to the feel of a traditional notebook or if you need grid lines for mathematical equations.

Top Feature #7

With OneNote you can take your notes "to go." By downloading the OneNote app on your Android or Apple iPhone, you can take all of your notes with you wherever you go. This is a great app to have because sometimes an idea can just hit you out of nowhere and it is important to be able to write it down immediately. The YouTube videos <u>OneNote on Any Device, Wherever You Are</u> by OfficeVideos and <u>Introduction to SkyDrive</u> by OneDrive are good starting points for learning how to sync and connect all of your devices.

Top Feature #8

Chances are that you may be keeping some personal information stored in a notebook on OneNote, such as your personal journal, account information, financial information, etc. OneNote has a password protection feature that allows you to guard off sections of your notebooks. You can lock a section of your notebook with a password by clicking on File and then **Password Protect This Section**.

Top Feature # 9

OneNote is extremely versatile. It is perfect so many different types of uses. If you practice all the features discussed in this book you should be easily able to organize your whole life into OneNote. Be sure to be creative. It is very easy to make a journal section by making each page a month and then just manually typing in the date of the journal entry. It may take a little effort at first to get OneNote to your satisfaction, but once you have done so... you will wonder why you ever had to go through all your previous torture before!

Conclusion

When used correctly, OneNote can be a powerful program. Think back to the last chapter where I explained to you how you can sync OneNote to all of your devices. I highly recommend setting this up as soon as you get OneNote (if you don't have it already). This way you will be prepared as soon as inspiration hits you or if you need to access your notes in a jiffy. Be sure to synchronize your personal computers, work computers and all mobile devices. You'll never know when you'll need to access your notes the most!

Here is an overview of all the neat things you can do with OneNote for ultimate organization and note-taking:

- Take notes without distractions.

- Use quick notes to write down urgent info. and file them later.

- Search all notes (typed, handwritten, audio/video) or individual pages/section with the search tools.

- Insert screen clippings from important documents to your notes.

- Use the Draw functions to take handwritten notes.

- Use the Draw functions to take handwritten notes over screen clippings, scanned images or other attachments.

- Make searchable tables and organize your information in them.

- Attach hyperlinks or file attachments to your tables for instant reference.

- Use the Linked Notes option to take notes with instant references attached.

- Create unlimited notes, pages, sections, etc.

- Never worry again about sifting through piles of loose papers or traditional notebooks ever again!

- Use the tags to mark important notes and check off boxes on your to-do lists for ultimate organization.

- Integrate OneNote with Outlook and SkyDrive for instant access anywhere.

- And much more! The creative possibilities are endless once you get to know the program.

If you're a businessperson who will also be using OneNote, I also recommend putting together an email list of all the people you will be in regular contact with. This can make it easier when you go to share your notebooks through email or the web. It can also ensure that you don't accidentally share your notebooks with the wrong person.

I hope this book was able to help you to understand and discover just how powerful and productive OneNote is!

The next step is to purchase OneNote (if you already have it), and just start playing around with it! I find that the best way to learn the ins and outs of a program is to just play around with it and explore each and every icon. Of course, you can also refer back to the chapters in this book for helpful advice. I can tell you OneNote has made my life as an author so much more efficient and organized! I have my whole personal and business life on OneNote and I have done my best to organize all this information the way a genius mastermind would do so. I urge you to do the same.

Finally, if you discovered at least one thing that has helped you or that you think would be beneficial to someone else, be sure to take a few seconds to easily post a quick positive review. As an author, your positive feedback is desperately needed. Your highly valuable five star reviews are like a river of golden joy flowing through a sunny forest of mighty trees and beautiful flowers! *To do your good deed in making the world a better place by helping others with your valuable insight, just leave a nice review.*

My Other Books and Audio Books
www.AcesEbooks.com

Business & Finance Books